JINGER VUOLO

BIOGRAPHY

HOW SHE
BECAME
FREE INDEED

COOPER ALDRIDGE

TABLE OF CONTENTS

Chapter 4

WHAT ARE JINGER AND JEREMY VUOLO REALLY LIKE?

Chapter 5

JINGER DUGGAR AND JEREMY VUOLO'S RELATIONSHIP TIMELINE

Chapter 7

15 THINGS THE DUGGARS DON'T LET THEIR DAUGHTERS DO

Chapter 8

JINGER VUOLO'S TRAGIC MOMENTS AND OUTBURSTS

Chapter 11

JINGER BEING IGNORED BY HER FAMILY BEFORE HER BOOK RELEASE

INTRODUCTION

In 2008, Jinger Duggar Vuolo and her family shot to fame thanks to the TLC show 19 Kids and Counting. In her new book, Becoming Free Indeed: My Story of Untangling Faith, she talks about how she went from being raised in a strict religion to finding the true meaning of God's word in the Bible.

The Duggar family's ultraconservative Christian lifestyle was portrayed on the TLC show 19 Kids and Counting until its cancellation in 2015. The Duggars were shown as following the controversial Christian beliefs of Bill Gothard, head of the Institute for Basic Life Principles (IBLP). They dressed modestly, taught their kids at home, and courted only under close supervision.

Growing Up Duggar was a book written by Vuolo and her three sisters, Jill, Jana, and Jessa, about the Duggar family's public, ultra-religious upbringing. In her first book under her own name, Duggar describes how she came to believe that young religion may be destructive, even a cover for abuse. Her newfound religious practice is described in the book as well, one that puts faith in God rather than in human leaders.

Vuolo was a staunch supporter of the IBLP back when the first season of 19 Kids aired. "I was definitely one of the most pious people in my family," she admits to PW. She cared deeply about setting an example for others on how to live a God-honoring life, and she tried to do so in everything from her wardrobe choices to the music she listened to. She found such lessons to be inspiring, and she believed that everyone should be exposed to them.

Jinger Vuolo says that her old religion was predicated on a dread of an angry God. "I was expecting God to judge me for stuff it says nothing about in the Bible," she admits. As the saying goes, "It nearly made me superstitious."

As she matured, she saw discrepancies in her beliefs. Many of Gothard's devotees never saw the material and relational rewards he promised them, despite their adherence to his every word. Even young children, as Vuolo observed, have trouble understanding Gothard's take on the Bible. She explains that her students learned "that we could never measure up to a flawless ideal of accomplishment."

In 2012, former members of the IBLP started publishing accounts of sexual abuse involving Gothard on a website called Recovering Grace, casting doubt on Gothard's own devotion to chastity and piety. He stepped down as president of the IBLP in 2014 after more than 30 women made charges against him and an internal inquiry was conducted. Ten of his accusers took legal action against him in 2016. The lawsuit was terminated in a formal manner in 2018.

It was also at this time that Vuolo's brother-in-law, Ben Seewald, exposed her to a different kind of religion. Seewald's congregation "studied the Bible in its entirety and taught it that way," as Vuolo put it after attending services there.

After just a year, Vuolo had begun to distance herself from the IBLP, and 19 Kids had ended in the midst of turmoil involving her own family. Due to allegations of sexual abuse against Vuolo's older brother, Josh, the program was terminated. Josh was arrested for child pornography in 2021, and the spin-off show Counting On kept following his parents, Jinger, and her other siblings after that.

In Becoming Free Indeed, Vuolo draws parallels between her brother Josh and Gothard to show how the disclosures affected her and strengthened her conviction that religious devotion comes from the inside rather than external performance. She now has two kids and lives in Los Angeles with her husband, Jeremy Vuolo, who used to play soccer for the United States.

Because of her status as a Gothardite, Vuolo is hoping that her new book will help her influence her former readers. The things she was told were harmful and inaccurate, she claims. Because she had advocated for ideas that she now finds harmful, she thought she had to make a public statement about them.

Six years of "disentangling truth from wrong" in Vuolo's interpretation of the Bible were well spent, she says. The last several days have put her in a much better frame of mind. God is really amazing in her eyes.

Associate publisher at W Publishing, Stephanie Newton, was moved by the book's hopeful message for those who have been damaged by religion and was attracted to publishing it. Vuolo "put in the effort to establish her own route ahead" after suffering wounds in childhood, as Newton puts it. We hope that this story will encourage other people to make an effort to make their religion more personal.

Vuolo agrees, adding that her narrative is meant to encourage others "who have fought with their religion" to "not give up on God."

Chapter 1

WHO IS JINGER DUGGAR VUOLO?

Her Early Life and Background

Jinger Duggar is a reality TV star and novelist who was born on December 21, 1993. Duggar is the fourth girl in a family of 19. "19 Kids and Counting," among other shows, was the film that catapulted her to fame to talk about her illustrious clan and its many members and unusual customs.

Jinger Nicole Duggar was born on December 21, 1995, to Michelle and Jim Bob Duggar in Fayetteville, Arkansas, as one of their 19 children. As the sixth kid overall, she is the fourth girl. Duggar and her older sister,

19

Jessa Seewald, are just 13 months apart in age. As a consequence of this, they have a unique bond.

To put it simply, Duggar grew up in a very religious Christian household. Her parents were the kind who thought it was important to teach their children good values and ethics. Duggar was barred from enrolling in a public institution of higher education after his conviction. She, like all her siblings, was instead home-schooled.

In addition, as one of the oldest children in the Duggar family, she was responsible for a number of domestic responsibilities, such as doing the washing and making the meals. Young Duggar also had an early passion for music, and she studied the violin and piano. In addition, she has an excellent grasp of the Bible.

In 2004, the documentary "14 Children and Pregnant Again" brought Duggar to widespread attention. At the time this film was being filmed, she was one of thirteen children. By 2006, they had added two more to their brood, and they were featured in a TV movie called "Raising 16 Children."

In addition to "Duggar's Big Family Album" (2008), "19 Kids and Counting" (2008), "Larry King Live" (2009), and "Counting On" (2015), Duggar has appeared in several other mediums. In 2015, she wrote the book

Growing Up Duggar with her sisters Jessa, Jana, and Jill.

Her parents gave their blessing that same year when she started dating Jeremy Vuolo, whom she had met. This pair finally tied the knot in 2016.

The Free Jinger Movement

When TLC's "19 Kids & Counting" was still airing, fans of the program and those who were not shared their opinions on the topic on the Free Jinger message boards. They did this because Jinger, out of Michelle and Jim Bob's 19 kids, always appeared the most inclined to break the rules and seek her own brand of "freedom."

Jinger understood this, since she was aware of the forum's existence from the start. The website's administrators "saw in me a girl they felt didn't have the good life because she didn't have uncontrolled freedom," Jinger reflected.

They believed she would find happiness if she was able to leave her family's extreme conservatism behind and choose her own path in life, including who to date, what kind of work to do, and even what and how much alcohol to drink.

Jinger Duggar On the Mental Health Toll of Being in The Public Eye

Jinger (Duggar) Vuolo discusses her experiences as a celebrity child. When

Jinger, now 29, was a child, her family started shooting for a Discovery Health Channel program that would eventually lead to their massively successful TLC series, 19 Kids and Counting, which ran from 2008 to 2015.

When her elder brother Josh Duggar was arrested on child pornography charges, she and many of her sisters became stars on the TLC reality show Counting On. The show was abruptly terminated in June 2021. By then, their brother had entered a not-guilty plea and gone to trial in November 2021.

The reality star talks about how fame has affected her mental health in an exclusive sneak peek of her interview on the podcast

Dinner Party with Jeremy Fall, which is hosted by Jeremy Fall and only available on PEOPLE. The podcast is made by Fall's company, JFALL, and is only available on People.

"Yes, like I'm saying, there are loads of rewards, but you also have to struggle with a lot," she added. She went on to say, "They might assume, 'Oh, you don't grapple with anything; you don't fight with being melancholy one day,' you know?" Or something like, "Your day hasn't gone as you'd hoped; how do you cope?" Going over that and learning how to actually open up to others has been more difficult for Jinger.

Jinger and her husband, Jeremy Vuolo, cling to their religion when times are tough, as she explains elsewhere in the radio episode. "We do all experience these emotions; we have periods when we're traveling through extremely tough, deep, dark times, and other people may not know about it or they may not realize that it's something that's universal to all humans," she added.

She continues, "We all go through obstacles and trials, and it is absolutely something I think about for us." "I believe that for me, at those moments when I struggle the most, I simply rush to God." "We are people of faith, and we have confidence in God."

Jinger has found it challenging to deal with the tabloid headlines and internet views about her family. As she puts it, "I cannot put up with what the tabloids are saying nowadays; I cannot put up with other people's ideas regarding even familial ties, what they say about my family." It hurts to hear that, but I remind myself: "Okay, wait, my identity is only found in Jesus Christ; my identity is not found in what people say about me today; my sense of self is not derived from any of these things; and because of who I am in Christ now, it doesn't matter."

Jinger, who has been married to Jeremy for some years and has two young daughters, Evangeline Jo and Felicity, believes that the paparazzi have a negative effect on her psyche, particularly now that she has kids and lives in Los Angeles rather than her home state of Arkansas. She recalls an incident in which a paparazzi attempted to photograph her family and yelled, "You put your kids on TV; come on, it's my right!"

She describes this so-called "regular act" as something that is really tough when you hear incorrect things stated about you or have the paparazzi pursuing you. Jinger claims that the pressure of being a public person has made her question whether or not she wants to be one at all. She adds that she never really had a choice in the issue since she was so young when 19 Kids and Counting premiered.

There have been several occasions on which she has expressed to Jeremy her desire to avoid the spotlight. She doesn't want outsiders peeking into their lives and judging them. As soon as she posts a picture of her family on Instagram, people will comment, "Oh, what a nice family picture!" In addition, some people will be cruel, even to your children. She's just two, and it's like, "Whoa!" Don't badmouth her, Jinger says, since "she can't even defend herself."

She adds, "There are days when I just wish I could say, 'Oh, no one knows who I am, ever again.'" But that will never be the case for Jinger Duggar, since her reputation precedes her. However, she is not always available online.

Chapter 2

HER CAREER AND EARNINGS

What Does Jinger Duggar Do?

Betting on her financial stability, Jinger Duggar has worked tirelessly in the positions of reality TV star and entrepreneur. Continue reading to learn about her income and assets.

Jinger wears several hats, including those of writer, podcaster, and business owner. In 2014, she published Growing Up Duggar: It's All About Relationships alongside her sisters Jana Duggar, Jill Duggar, and Jessa Duggar. In May 2021, Jinger and her husband, Jeremy Vuolo, released their second book, The Hope We Hold: Finding Peace with the Promises of God.

The former reality star's first children's book, co-written with Jeremy and featuring artwork by Naomi C. Robinson, was released in August 2022 with the title "You Can Shine So Bright!" Jinger, on the other hand, isn't putting down the pen anytime soon. On January 31, 2023, she releases a new book titled Becoming Free Indeed.

In her new book, the former TLC star recounts how she started to question the damaging ideals of her upbringing and learned to embrace genuine freedom in Christ, as the book's blurb puts it. The November 2022 issue of In Touch magazine had an exclusive interview with a source who said that Jinger's parents, Jim Bob and Michelle Duggar, were "bracing themselves" for the effect of their daughter's honesty on paper.

Someone close to the family said, "Jim Bob and Michelle aren't delighted about Jinger's book coming out, but they are praying for the best." They have prayed about it and hope that it is honest, polite, and doesn't dig up too much of their family difficulties, but they don't know what themes she'll touch.

The author and mother of two announced on November 1, 2022, on Instagram that she will be collaborating with Matchbox Coffee to produce a new coffee mix. She posted a video on Instagram showing her making the coffee mix with the caption, "I've wanted to do this for years and finally did."

Jinger's consistent promotion of Matchbox Coffee on her Instagram feed probably didn't catch followers off guard when they heard about the connection. She and Jeremy also present the podcast "The Hope We Hold."

How Does Jinger Duggar Make Money?

Likely, Jinger's initial source of income came from appearing on a number of TLC reality series with her renowned family. In 2008, she first appeared in the MTV reality series that would eventually become known as 17 Kids and Counting, then 18 Kids and Counting, and now 19 Kids and Counting.

Due to the molestation controversy involving Josh Duggar, the program was terminated in 2015, although some of the Duggars went on to feature in the spinoff Counting On, which will air from 2015 to 2020.

The network stated in April 2021 that it would no longer produce fresh episodes of the family program after Josh was arrested on child pornography allegations. TLC has decided not to renew Counting On for a new season. "TLC thinks it is vital to offer the Duggar family the chance to handle their problem quietly," the network told Us Weekly in June.

After a nine-day trial in December 2021, an Arkansas jury convicted the oldest Duggar kid guilty of receiving child pornography and having child pornography. At his sentencing, the judge decided not to include the child pornography possession allegation.

On May 25, the disgraced reality star was handed a jail term of almost 12.5 years. His original release date was July 12, 2020; however, In Touch stated in July that it had been moved to August 12, 2032, which is a little more than 10 years.

What Is Jinger Duggar's Net Worth?

Jinger Duggar makes her own money through paid promotion on social media, which is another source of income for her. She has worked with companies such as Good Ranchers and Uber Eats to advertise their goods to her 1.4 million Instagram followers.

According to Celebrity Net Worth, Jinger is estimated to have a net worth of $2 million at the present time.

Chapter 3

JINGER DUGGAR'S HUSBAND

Who Is Jeremy Joseph Vuolo?

Jeremy Joseph Vuolo, born in the United States on September 5, 1987, played for MLS and the NASL. After marrying Jinger Duggar (one of the 19 Duggar children in 19 Kids and Counting), he appears in the spinoff series Counting On.

Vuolo is the child of Chuck and Diana Vuolo, and he was born in Philadelphia. He went to Downingtown West High School and got a degree in business management from Hartwick College in 2010. Vuolo started playing collegiate soccer in 2006 at

Hartwick College before moving to Syracuse University in 2010 to finish his final year.

Before and during college, Vuolo also featured for PDL team Reading United between 2005 and 2010. Vuolo joined the Finnish club AC Oulu after graduating from college, and he ended up playing in 24 games for them, keeping 11 clean sheets. In 2012, Vuolo signed with the New York Red Bulls of Major League Soccer, marking his return to the United States.

Following his release from New York, Vuolo took some time away from soccer to devote himself to full-time ministry. However, in April of 2013, he revealed that he had signed with the NASL's San Antonio Scorpions.

There is no evidence that he was still listed as an active player for the NASL beyond June of 2016.

In 2016, Vuolo married the famous reality star Jinger Duggar. Felicity and Evangeline are their two offspring. His faith is Christian.

How Much Did Jinger Duggar's Husband Make as A Soccer Player?

Jeremy Vuolo was a professional soccer player before he met Jinger Duggar; however, he apparently didn't earn a fortune in that field. Over the years, the media has paid a lot of attention to the Duggar family because of how they live and what their oldest child has done.

There are, however, Duggar followers who aren't interested in the family itself but in the husbands of the daughters. In this case, Jeremy Vuolo in particular. The former soccer player is the most libertine of the Duggar wives since he doesn't share the same morals and values as the rest of the family.

However, Jeremy Vuolo does not seem to be a very wealthy or famous person. Also, he doesn't seem to be earning any money from his employment right now. Regardless of how much the Duggar spouse is making now, or not at all, here's how much he earned as a professional soccer player.

Was Jeremy Vuolo a Pro MLS Soccer Player?

Jeremy Vuolo played soccer for Major League Soccer and the North American Soccer League before he married the renowned Jinger Duggar. The vast majority of people are aware of this reality. In 2006, Vuolo first stepped onto a collegiate soccer field. He later graduated in 2010 with a Business Administration degree.

After spending time with a few different clubs, he made it to the NASL, where he could play professional soccer. Jeremy's professional career spans from 2012, when he was with the New York Red Bulls, through 2014, when he was with the Scorpions.

By 2016, it seemed that Jeremy had given up on a career in professional soccer to devote himself full-time to the ministry. In the same year, he tied the knot with Jinger Duggar. Fans of the Duggar family were astonished when Jinger started dating Jeremy, particularly in light of his less-than-strict upbringing.

Naturally, no Duggar would ever consider making a living as a professional soccer player. But Jeremy appears to have impressed the Duggar parents with his account of how his life had altered as a result of his religious development, and he and Jinger seem to be content in their marriage today.

However, this does not imply that Jeremy is sorry he spent so much time playing soccer. On Instagram in 2022, he's tagged the New York Red Bulls and the San Antonio Scorpions with a soccer ball emoji.

How Much Is Jeremy Vuolo Worth?

As a result of his popularity, fans may assume that Jeremy Vuolo was wealthy before he met and married Jinger Duggar. The money he was thought to have at the time may not have been as plentiful as previously believed. After graduating from college, Jeremy pursued soccer as a career, but he was never able to earn multimillion-dollar salaries like Cristiano Ronaldo or Lionel Messi.

The estimates of his pay from several sources suggest that it was likely rather low. Celebrity Net Worth estimates Jeremy Vuolo has a current net worth of $2 million; however, it's not clear how much of it comes from his soccer career.

Jeremy Vuolo is also said to have never played for the New York Red Bulls, even though he was on the roster for 20 games while he was with the Scorpions.

How Much Did Jeremy Vuolo Make Playing Soccer?

According to available data, Jeremy Vuolo spent the most of his (paid) soccer career with the San Antonio Scorpions. From what I can tell, the Scorpions play in the North American Soccer League, which doesn't seem to disclose player pay to the general public.

But soccer fans have made educated guesses about player salaries in online forums based on a number of factors. An NASL official indicated the players' monthly salaries ranged from $2,700 to $3,200 in 2013, according to a commenter who saw the pay information presented during a live game.

This cap would put your annual salary at slightly over $38,000.

In a discussion comparing the NASL and MLS, one fan said, "Till now, there is nothing more definite than wild speculation as to the salary of players in the second and third divisions of the US soccer pyramid" (Major League Soccer). Unless they're superstars who presumably make $100K or more, the general opinion on that thread was that players in both divisions made between $40,000 and $60,000 annually.

In conclusion? Jeremy Vuolo didn't get rich playing soccer.

How Does Jeremy Vuolo Make Money Now?

So far as Jeremy knows, his career as a theologian (pastor) is not paying well financially. According to the cheat sheet, Jinger earns between $100,000 and $200,000 every year owing to her social media presence and other ventures, including her books.

Although the family's reality TV income has dried up since "Counting On" was cancelled, Jinger continues to support the household financially so that her husband may follow his religious interests.

And who knows, maybe one day Jeremy will have a well-paying position in the church.

There's also the possibility that Jinger may remain the primary earner in the family. We think that's a first for the Duggars!

"The Truman Show": The First Movie Jinger and Jeremy Watched Together

Previewing her forthcoming book, Becoming Free Indeed, Vuolo reveals that she and her husband, Jeremy Vuolo, first viewed The Truman Show. While on their honeymoon in Australia, the happy couple attended a screening of the film. The experience left an indelible mark on Jinger's psyche.

The reality TV star and author said she turned to her husband as the film ended and said, "That was me!" Jinger is correct in many respects. Growing up, Truman

Burbank (Tom Hanks) watches TV. Equally, Jinger Vuolo did. In the film, viewers were always giving Truman advice on how to conduct his life.

As the Duggars became a staple of TLC programming, many fans began formulating opinions about the family and its children. If you're a fan of the Duggar family, the analogy works just as well. Nearly everyone agrees that Jinger's story parallels that of Truman Burbank in many respects.

They don't think for a second that it was a coincidence that they played The Truman Show first. Skeptics of the Duggar family say it's no coincidence.

Do Followers Think the Movie Choice Was a Coincidence?

Immediately after Jinger's book teaser was made public, fans of the Duggar family flocked to Reddit to debate the new information. Some of her devotees singled out her "Truman Show" recounting. One commenter insisted that picking that particular film couldn't have been a coincidence.

Several others also shared the opinion that Jeremy Vuolo was eager to expose the Duggars whenever the chance presented itself. As far as Duggar courtships go, Jeremy and Jinger's were far from smooth. If you ask Jim Bob Duggar, he probably wouldn't have picked Jeremy as his first option for his daughter.

Jinger described her internal turmoil about starting a romance with Jeremy in the couple's first book, "The Hope We Hold." She feared that moving ahead would cause strife among her loved ones, as she explained. The two did end up getting married, however. After being married, Jinger quickly relocated to Jeremy's pastorate in Laredo, Texas.

Since then, they've expanded their family to include two children, settled in Los Angeles, and bought a house. There are rumors that the move and Jinger's desire to wear pants and live a more global life have made things worse between her and her parents.

It's possible that Jeremy Vuolo's decision to show his wife "The Truman Show" wasn't as deliberate as some Duggar family fans may have you believe. Someone from Australia posting on Reddit said the video was widely shown throughout the honeymoon. The commenter said that they, too, recalled viewing the film in November of 2016.

They even exchanged schedules to demonstrate that the film was screened during the couple's visit to the country. That doesn't rule out the possibility that Jeremy made a deliberate decision. No doubt there were other movies to choose from than The Truman Show that day.

The publication date of Becoming Free Indeed, the new book by Jinger Vuolo, is January 31, 2023. Vuolo is unlikely to discuss the internal politics of the Duggar family, but she does offer an intimate glimpse at her life as a former reality TV star. Her breakup with the IBLP and her experience on TLC will also be addressed in the book.

In the past few years, members of Jinger's family have also moved away from the controversial ministry, so she is not the only one.

Chapter 4

WHAT ARE JINGER AND JEREMY VUOLO REALLY LIKE?

There's little doubt that Jim Bob and Michelle Duggar followed a strict set of guidelines in raising their daughters, and the conservative family was more than willing to broadcast those guidelines to the rest of the world. Fans of the Duggar family's reality program have seen the nineteen children, including Jinger, mature over the years, and several of them are now married parents.

Many of the children of the Duggars have gone on to choose their own paths in life, distinct from those of their parents, but none have gone so far as Jinger. She is the most beautiful and the real outsider of the Duggar family, and she and her husband, Jeremy Vuolo, refuse to fit in with what society expects of them.

See what it's like behind the scenes with this real-life pair.

The Vuolos Relax Differently Than Their Brothers and Sisters

While growing up, Duggar children were subject to the rigorous guidelines put down by their parents. One such regulation concerned the kind of media to which the children were allowed access. The parents of the Duggar children have banned almost all TV shows because they don't want their kids to be exposed to violence, sexual content, or other things that could be bad for them.

In contrast, Jinger and Jeremy are not averse to a little TV since they find it soothing. The English Game, The Great British Bake Off, and Madam Secretary are some of Jinger's all-time favorite shows.

The Couple Didn't Jump Right into Parenthood.

Rather than dating, the Duggar children were taught to court. Jinger, like her siblings before her, courted and married her future husband. She was different in that she and her husband, Jeremy, waited a while before starting a family after getting married.

Once again, Jinger goes her own way, and we admire her for that!

They Are Not Neighbors with Jim, Bob, And Michelle—Not Even Close.

It's safe to assume that the nineteen Duggar kids spent a lot of time together growing up, what with them all sharing a house and being homeschooled. Most of the children have stayed close to Jim Bob and Michelle Duggar as they've grown up, but Jinger and her family have drifted apart.

They upped and moved out to Laredo from Arkansas in order to set down permanent roots. Jinger and Jeremy just moved again, this time to sunny California, far from where Jinger grew up in a small town in the Midwest.

Getting A Good Education

Jeremy Vuolo, Jinger's spouse, played soccer at both Hartwick College and the University of Syracuse. He left it all behind to pursue a new interest in religion, married Jinger, and is just now getting back into the academic realm.

The reason Jeremy and his family just relocated to the Los Angeles region was so that he could finish his master's degree at the Master's Seminary. Jinger, for her part, seems happy tending to her domestic duties.

Jinger Is the Family Fashion Rebel, And Her Husband Approves.

Jinger Vuolo has been known as the family's resident renegade. She still has deep roots in her religion, but she is not afraid to make adjustments to the strict norms she was brought up with. Daughters of the Duggars were usually seen dressed modestly, with long skirts or other garments that covered almost all of their bodies.

Jinger has recently embraced jeans, t-shirts, shorter skirts, and even shorts! Jinger hasn't stopped experimenting with her wardrobe. In addition to that, she's gone and altered the color of her hair from brown to blonde.

They Enjoy Traveling.

Both Jinger and Jeremy Vuolo like exploring new places, but Jeremy is especially fond of traveling. They are the pair that uprooted their lives from a little hamlet and planted them firmly in a major American metropolis. When they have leisure time, they like going to other locations.

After being married in the Midwest, they had their honeymoon in Australia and subsequently relocated to the South and now the Far West. Who knows where life will take this young couple and their children?

Life Isn't Always Sunny: Jinger, Like Sister Joy, Has Had a Miscarriage.

The Duggar girls have certainly experienced heartbreak. The first of Michelle's pregnancies ended in miscarriage decades ago, and her second ended in the same way in 2014. Joy, Jinger's sister, also had a miscarriage after giving birth to a boy.

Jinger and Jeremy only recently spoke out about the fact that Jinger miscarried before becoming pregnant with their daughter. The Vuolos went through a difficult time with the loss, so they are really appreciative of their healthy newborn.

She looks like she's becoming big and powerful in her mother's tummy.

Unlike The Other Duggar Children, They Appear Determined to Raise Felicity.

Compared to Jinger's other siblings, who are also parents, the Vuolos take a different approach. Though the Duggars don't often watch TV at home, the Vuolos do, and they have favorites! We assume that they do not mind if Felicity, at her young age, watches a TV episode or two now and again.

Jinger took a photo of her daughter talking on the phone lately. Both of them seem to be more receptive to modern technologies and have a more laid-back lifestyle than the majority of the Duggar clan.

They Got Their Start Uniquely, Compared to Their Siblings

Since becoming a couple, these two have done everything in their own way. It was via Jinger's brother-in-law, Ben Seewald, that the two of them first connected. Unlike the other Duggar guys who "married in," Jeremy had already lived a complete life full of partying and college life.

While Jinger and Jeremy followed most of the Duggars' prescribed wooing procedures, they did break the rules one or twice by engaging in full-on front embraces. We hate picking favorites, but if we had to choose our favorite Duggar family, it would be this one.

Chapter 5

JINGER DUGGAR AND JEREMY VUOLO'S RELATIONSHIP TIMELINE

They showed the world what real love looks like on Counting On. Jinger Duggar and Jeremy Vuolo quickly fell in love with one another and made each other their priority from the beginning of their romance until the birth of their children. Their romance undoubtedly developed rapidly, but it is also deeply rooted.

Jinger and Jeremy have an incredible love story, and we're going to tell it here. This couple showed the world what kind of love is possible on Counting On. It's an example worth following and a source of motivation for individuals of all backgrounds.

65

Let's get into Jinger and Jeremy's long and winding love story without further ado!

2015

Because of his friendship with Jinger's brother-in-law Ben, Jeremy Vuolo visited the Duggar family in Arkansas and then accompanied Jinger on a mission trip to Central America. But he needed Jim Bob's OK to start wooing his future bride.

Jim Bob, according to Vuolo, had him fill out a rigorous 50-page questionnaire to demonstrate his devotion to Jinger. Jinger writes on the early phases of her spark with Jeremy in their new biography, The Hope

We Hold, admitting that she "had never felt such a strong attraction to anybody."

July 2016

Jeremy and Jinger didn't spend any time getting to know one another; they got engaged in July 2016 in New York City. Jinger and Jeremy are excited about serving Christ together in the days ahead, as stated in their blog post, and they are so happy for how the Lord has brought them together.

November 2016

The couple tied the knot in Arkansas in front of close to a thousand friends and family members at the Cathedral of the

Ozarks on the campus of John Brown University, three months after becoming engaged in November 2016.

Before they were married, Jinger and Jeremy said there were times when they weren't sure whether their relationship would last, stating, "There were a few ups and downs."

November 2017

Once the reality TV actress and her husband had been married for a year, she posted a gorgeous wedding picture of the two of them on Instagram. Vuolo marked the event with a beautiful self-portrait on

Instagram, which was almost as good as the picture taken at their wedding.

They are the epitome of #couplegoals and seem as in love as ever.

July 2018

On July 19, 2018, the couple had their first child, a daughter named Felicity Nicole. If you've been keeping up with Jinger and Jeremy on Instagram, you already know what a fortunate girl Felicity is.

If you didn't know they had a social media platform, you should check it out immediately.

May 2020

Jinger's second pregnancy was announced on social media, and the couple were clearly overjoyed. They revealed their happy news along with the sad news that Jinger suffered a miscarriage while trying for a second child.

On Instagram, Jeremy Vuolo said, "Life is amazing!" along with "We are thanking God for this wonderful gift."

November 2020

Jinger's second child was born shortly after she spoke out about her previous loss. According to Jinger's Instagram post, the name Evangeline Jo was chosen for the couple's rainbow baby since it combines two of Jeremy's middle name's initials.

They've also acknowledged that it's been challenging to bring up their kids in the spotlight.

May 2021

The cute couple spent Mother's Day having lunch and taking things easy. Jinger posted a sweet photo of herself and Jeremy on Instagram and wished all the amazing mothers out there a happy Mother's Day.

June 2021

As a final note, here's maybe the sweetest part of the whole thing. After sharing a photo of his wife without any makeup on Instagram, Vuolo exclaimed, "I truly like her." So basic, but so indicative of their deep affection for one another!

Even though the public has become rather attached to the amazing foursome, they will no longer be shown on TLC. After Josh Duggar's arrest two months earlier caused a big stir, the network announced in June 2021 that they were ending Counting On.

After hearing the cancellation news, the couple took to Instagram to express their gratitude to TLC for the chance to be on the network throughout the years and for their compassion toward the Vuolo family. The show has been amazing and has given them the opportunity to see the globe in ways they never thought possible.

The couples were in support of TLC's decision not to renew Counting On, as they look forward to moving on to the next phase of their lives. It's unfortunate that we are not seeing the happy family on TV any more, but I suppose that everything happens for a reason.

You can get your Jinger and Jeremy fix by following them on Instagram.

Jinger (Duggar) Vuolo and Her Husband Relocating to Los Angeles.

Jeremy and Jinger (Duggar) Vuolo relocated to the West Coast. The "Counting On" star and Vuolo, a former professional soccer player turned preacher, relocated from Laredo, Texas, to Los Angeles. Leaving Laredo in July 2019 was one of the toughest things they have ever done, despite how much they are looking forward to their new journey. Their friends here have become like family. They were in need of prayers as they began the new phase of their lives.

Jinger moved from her hometown of Little Rock, Arkansas, to Laredo, Texas, with her husband Jeremy in November 2016 after they were married. On July 19, 2018, the couple, who had just relocated to Texas, became parents for the first time to a girl whom they called Felicity Nicole.

Jeremy said at the moment, "God is so nice." "Mom and baby are doing wonderful; they are both in good health and receiving the necessary amount of rest." We are very grateful that she made it here safely and are excited to start our new lives as parents.

Jinger and Jeremy Celebrating Their Seventh Wedding Anniversary.

Seven years ago today, Jinger (Duggar) Vuolo said, "I do." Jinger, now 29 years old, paid Instagram's Friday anniversary tribute to her husband, Jeremy Vuolo. She posted a slideshow of wedding photos with a caption. In 2016, Duggar wed Vuolo at John Brown University's Cathedral of the Ozarks in Siloam Springs, Arkansas. They posted the good news on their website not long after the wedding.

"YES! That does it for us; we're hitched! "We love that we are now starting our lives together as one before God," the couple said at the time. "We are so appreciative to God, our parents, and our amazing families and friends for enjoying this day with us and helping us arrive at this moment."

Jessa Duggar (Seewald), another Duggar sister who just had an anniversary, was the one who introduced Vuolo to Duggar. Ben Seewald, Jessa's husband, knew Vuolo and was friendly with him. The courtship between Duggar and Vuolo started in 2015, after a mission trip they took together.

After waiting another month, they finally broke the news that they were engaged. The Vuolos have two little daughters: Evangeline, who is two years old, and Felicity, who is four years old. The couple had more to rejoice about than just their anniversary.

According to both, when they tuck their daughters into bed each night, they read them a tale. It's become one of their favorite parts of the day! Duggar posted on the Instagram social media platform. "The drawings are Evy Jo's favorite part, and Felicity enjoys hearing about all the other characters." It's been a blast and a dream come true to be able to create a book for their daughters and for kids all across the globe.

Chapter 6

10 JUICY FACTS ABOUT OUR FAVORITE DUGGAR, JINGER

Jinger Duggar, now Vuolo, has emerged as the most popular of the Duggar children. There is no shortage of colorful personalities in the Duggar household. We've learned a lot about the kids' (there are nineteen of them) interests, quirks, and even dark secrets as they've grown older.

Here are some interesting facts about her you may never have known prior to reading this book.

Her Sense of Humor Is Dark and Snarky.

Count us as lifelong fans of Jinger if the shade she threw at her parents by wearing a blouse that says "Nike" is any indication of her wit and attitude. When the Duggar children were younger, there was a secret name for when a woman in skimpy clothing strolled by.

Jinger was once seen on camera not only wearing trousers but also a Nike t-shirt, which caused widespread outrage. Maybe she was nodding in reference to that crazy rule in her family. Certainly, that's the hope, anyhow.

Jinger Could Have Courted Her Husband Before Marrying Him.

When it comes to dating, the Duggars have a lot of rules, many of which center on the idea of courtship. When Duggars go on dates, it's with the goal of getting engaged and eventually getting married. Jinger and her husband Jeremy Vuolo have been married for some time now, but before Jeremy, there was Lawson Bates.

Considering how close the Bates and Duggar families are, it's only natural that their children would get romantically involved. Although Jinger and Lawson were seen on camera during her cousin Amy's wedding, following the festivities, Jinger's focus shifted to her now-husband Jeremy.

Truthfully, no one can blame Lawson for trying to woo Jinger. Look at her Instagram—she's gorgeous.

She May Be a Rebel, But She Is Not Going to Cut Her Hair.

Jinger Duggar is not planning to cut her hair really short, which is just one of the many surprising things about Jinger that have her supporters scratching their heads. The Duggar sisters' guide says that a woman's hair is her crowning feature, so cutting it short is the worst thing you can do.

She may be the most progressive Duggar daughter, wearing slacks and skirts and delaying motherhood, but even she won't go as far as to shave her head. The future, however, is uncertain now that Jinger has shown her locks.

Country-Born, City-Dwelling

Most of the Duggar children still reside in the tiny, conservative Midwestern villages where they were born and raised. The only Duggar child who ever wanted to make it big was Jinger. She wanted to leave her hometown after marrying Jeremy Vuolo; therefore, she made that move.

Rather than New York City, Jeremy took her to Laredo, Texas, before finally ending up in sunny California. What an incredible thought! money to cover basic expenses from the Duggars, the wealthiest family in Hollywood.

Her Father Might Not Have Been a Big Fan of Her Boyfriend.

Big Jim Bob Duggar, Jinger's father, is notorious for manipulating his family members and dictating their romantic partnerships. Jim Bob's tight relationship with Michelle continues even after their children are grown.

Jinger and Jeremy are their own individuals, and Jim Bob is not allowed into

84

their relationship. However, Jim Bob may have had a role in setting up several of his children and directing them after they were married.

It has been said that Jim Bob does not like Jeremy Vuolo very much, and that this is because Jeremy is not as malleable as his other children, business partners, or marriage partners.

Jinger Enjoys Listening to Secular Music.

As a result of Jim Bob and Michelle Duggar's restrictive parenting, the Duggar children did not have many opportunities to explore and learn. They weren't permitted to wear whatever they wanted, and females weren't allowed to cut their hair.

Neither group was able to participate in organized sports or go to public school. They also weren't allowed to partake in activities like dancing, watching TV, or listening to pop music.

Jinger no longer feels any shame when she dances to a fun song on the radio now that she is a mature lady, a wife, and a mother.

Jinger and Her Husband Do Not Follow the Duggars' Religion

The Duggars are a devout Christian family who have instilled their faith in their children. Because Jeremy Vuolo is a pastor,

Jinger now has a husband who shares her religious beliefs. However, the Vuolos' religion is different from the one Jinger was raised in.

Jeremy is a Christian fundamentalist, but his brand of Christianity is unique. Jinger and her siblings were brought up in a very conservative Baptist home. There is no inherent conflict between the two worldviews, but we can't imagine Jim Bob accepting his daughter's conversion lightly.

She Struggled with Motherhood.

When people think of parenting, they think of the Duggars. The young adults mature, find partners, and start families within 10 minutes after exchanging vows. In this aspect, Jinger is unique. The couple had already been married for some time before they decided to share the news that they were expecting.

The second is that Jinger struggled to adjust to her new role as a mother. To the contrary, she found it intimidating at first. After this bombshell dropped, the Counting On cast spoke about becoming pregnant and becoming a mother. This honesty is exactly what we've been looking for.

Her Hobby Pushed the Boundaries of Stereotypes.

Children raised in a Duggar household are expected to adhere to rigid gender roles.

There is little deviation from the norms established by one's parents and faith, regardless of one's gender. Boys are encouraged to pursue one set of interests, while girls are encouraged to pursue another.

We find it intriguing that Jinger has taken up the traditionally male-dominated activity of automobile flipping. Jinger is proving herself to be one of the most creative members of the Duggar family with her bike renovations and photography.

Jinger Might Enjoy the Occasional Adult Beverage

Although Jinger and Jeremy have never publicly admitted to being cocktail enthusiasts, it has been reported that the wait staff at a certain restaurant handed Jinger a bubbly alcoholic drink while her spouse sipped on a beer. The Duggars, as a rule, are abstainers.

It's just one of the many rules the Duggar children are taught to follow. Well, our lady Jinger is the one who's going to give it a go on her own terms, so she has her own life to live now.

Chapter 7

15 THINGS THE DUGGARS DON'T LET THEIR DAUGHTERS DO

Jim Bob is a very strict parent, particularly when it comes to the regulations he imposes on his daughters. We have seen the age and size of the Duggar family expand throughout the years. TLC's "19 Kids & Counting" and its spinoff "Counting On" have given us a front-row seat to the happy ending of one family: we've seen the kids find love, get married, and start their own families.

Jim Bob has some rather rigid standards for his children, particularly his daughters. This man takes the rules extremely seriously and will punish anyone who

91

disobeys them. However, it seems that not all of his offspring share his strict interpretation of these laws, since some of them have been caught breaking them in the past.

Here are 15 things that female Duggars can't do before or after getting engaged, and 5 things that they can do.

No Dating Without a Chaperone

Double dates are a tradition in this household. The Duggar parents are said to often engage in double dating with their offspring. They are taking this precaution to ensure that their children will not disobey the regulations.

In the event that both parents are unable to go, an older sibling is often sent in their place.

No Private Text Messages

Parents have been known to snoop on their children's text messages since the invention of mobile phones. Jim Duggar reads all of his daughters' communications.

When Ben Seewald asked Jessa to give him a ring in a message, Jim chimed in to say, "No ring yet," with a winking emoji.

Divorce Is Never an Option.

After the couple has exchanged their "I do" vows, they can no longer back out of their commitment. The Duggar family plans to stay together for the foreseeable future.

After the Josh Duggar affair, for instance, nobody could bring up divorce. Anna, his wife, even tried to take the blame for him.

Co-Ed Hide and Seek Is Now a No-No.

A controversy involving Josh Duggar, one of Jim Bob's kids, made headlines a few years ago. Jim altered several family policies as a result of the affair. One of the rules he instituted was that kids of both sexes were no longer allowed to play outside together in games of hide-and-seek.

There Is No Obvious Party.

It's quite evident that this is the correct answer. In general, parents don't want their kids going out drinking and partying. The Duggars' greatest vice is indulging in sweet desserts every once in a while and generally basking in the euphoria of their many happy relationships and the adoration of their adoring fans.

Love Stories Are Off-Limits for Them to Read.

The Duggar children are not allowed to read romance novels or any other genre that may influence them. The Bible says we shouldn't "think about satisfying the pleasures of the flesh." Their parents think this means it's wrong to read romance books.

In its place, the family reads a wide variety of Christian works.

Dancing and Modern Music Promote Bad Habits.

Michelle Duggar is the family matriarch. She thinks that modern music makes young children feel "sensual," so she doesn't let them listen to it or dance to it. Michelle believes that today's music and dance encourage all of the wrong behaviors in children.

That's why they listen exclusively to Christian music in the car.

They Must Cover Up When Swimming and Aren't Allowed to Ever Go to The Beach.

The Duggars follow the rule that it's best to be very careful when going out on the water. Women are not only forbidden from using the beach, but they are also required to cover themselves while swimming because men cannot look away.

When it comes to gatherings, one particular family insists on only having pool parties.

It's Against the Rules to Have One-On-One Phone Conversations with Boys.

The Duggar parents are known to keep tabs on their children's phone conversations just as closely as they do their children's text messages. Jim, Bob, and Michelle listen in on all incoming and outgoing phone calls.

Some of their offspring apparently aren't on board with this regulation and have acted dishonestly behind their parents' backs. Jessa Duggar, one of the Duggars, said that she had an affair with Ben Seewald before the two of them got engaged.

They Are Not Permitted to Celebrate Halloween Because It Is a Demonic Holiday.

These days, Halloween is all about wild parties, hot costumes, and exciting tricks. Even if all of the wrongdoings were cleared, the Duggar family would refuse to appear.

Jim Bob and Michelle Duggar think that sorcery, witchcraft, and other magical creatures live in the world of the demons.

They Are Not Allowed to Turn Down Their Husbands.

Michelle made it a point to teach her girls the advice her own mother had given her: never say "no" to your future husband or wife.

There are widespread claims that wives should never say "no," should always be happy, and should be there for their husbands even when they are too busy, too fatigued, or too obviously pregnant to care.

No Worldly Content Is Allowed.

In the summer of 2015, Jim Bob sent a letter to every parent on the planet, telling them to do a better job of keeping their families safe by restricting their children's access to harmful media, including books, magazines, television, and the internet.

According to him, parents should only let their kids listen to Christian music, read biographies of famous Christians, play traditional family games, and do other family-friendly things.

Communication with Unwed Mothers Is Against the Rules, Even If They Are Family.

When it comes to their views on sexual activity before marriage, the Duggars are fiercely committed to one another. The Kellers didn't want their midwife daughter, Jill, to help her pregnant sister, Susanne Keller, who was carrying an illegitimate child.

Jill didn't need to see her single mother, so that was OK with the Duggars.

It Is Prohibited to Seek Therapy from an Outside Therapist.

The Duggar parents thought it was better to deal with the Josh Duggar controversy internally. They sent him to Reformers Unanimous, a faith-based recovery program that is Christ-centered and aims to rescue, rehabilitate, and restore a person with addictive tendencies, rather than calling the authorities and getting professional treatment.

No Birth Control?

So, this has never been a rule for the women in the house, but it is very clear that it has never been put into practice. It is not uncommon for couples to start a family soon after exchanging wedding vows. It would seem that they are always, if not permanently, expecting.

They Are Allowed to Have Their Own Social Media Accounts After Marriage.

Once they are married, the restriction no longer applies, just as it did for hand-holding, frontal embraces, chaperones on dates, and having a third person sit in the middle of the vehicle at all times.

After getting married, women are finally permitted to have their own social media profiles. They will likely share many heartwarming photos of their expanding family.

They Are Permitted to Hold Hands After They Have Been Engaged.

At first, the Duggar parents don't think it's right for a young couple to hold hands or hug each other in front. Young couples' danger level goes from zero to one hundred the moment they start holding hands.

Hence, it is forbidden until the pair is engaged.

They Are Permitted to Perform Chest-To-Chest Hugs Once Married.

The Duggar daughters are only allowed to give each other side hugs while interacting with people of the opposite gender. "Hanky-panky" or other sexually suggestive behavior may follow a full-frontal embrace. So they only let their kids hug on the side to keep them from being tempted.

After their daughters get married, though, they are free to give their husbands a big chest-to-chest squeeze.

They Are Permitted to Minister to Prisoners in Prison.

Okay, so this one's a stretch. However, the Duggars' children were allowed to interact with inmates but not with their sister, who had a child outside of marriage. H.M. Jinger and Jessa occasionally go to Florida prisons to preach to the inmates.

After The Engagement, Middlemen in Cars Are No Longer Required.

The Duggar girls are not permitted to ride alone in a vehicle with a potential suitor of the other sex when they are on a date. They always have to bring a family member along whenever they go out with their boyfriend.

Once a proposal is made, this regulation is no longer relevant. although they are still not allowed to engage in sexually improper contact.

Chapter 8

JINGER VUOLO'S TRAGIC MOMENTS AND OUTBURSTS

Her 18-Hour Labor with Baby Felicity

As Jinger (Duggar) Vuolo got ready for the birth of her child, she put her daughter's health and safety first. On Monday's episode of "Counting On," viewers saw Jinger and Jeremy Vuolo become parents for the first time to their daughter Felicity Nicole Vuolo. Prior to her birth, Jinger and Jeremy went to a birthing facility for a prenatal checkup and talked to their midwife, Alisa.

Because her sisters had had such enormous kids that they felt it would be better if she sort of got closer to her due date, Jinger's doctor and midwife recommended that she give birth early. They wanted to induce her, so she packed up the vehicle with everything she needed, including the baby's car seat. It's surreal to think that she was soon going to hold her newborn in her arms.

Jinger would walk three miles a day and perform more than 100 squats to get her body ready for birth. That's why she's been engaging in what we call "natural nudging." According to her doctor, "Jinger has been taking certain herbs to help her body get ready, and she's been walking and doing things to assist the baby in coming into a healthy position."

Based on family history, some of the sisters have had a little bit of a tougher time with larger infants. Jinger, Jeremy, and her doctor have discussed at length about trying to keep a baby's size a little bit lower and maybe seeing if the kid might arrive closer to the due date rather than going a week or two over.

Following her doctor's visit, Jinger stated, "to continue tonight with more herbs, walking, and if things move forward, then simply heading to the hospital, I suppose, and beginning some inducing." Jinger and Jeremy chose a hospital delivery rather than a home birth, which she claimed made her feel at peace.

Furthermore, Jinger opted to give birth at a hospital since several of her sisters have gone through a bit of a terrible time with labor and delivery. In her further explanation, it just sort of puts her at ease knowing that, well, if she needs something, it's here. She anticipates a greater sense of calm as a result.

Jinger checked into the hospital on July 17, 2018, and on July 18, she was given Pitocin, a medicine used to induce labor by stimulating or increasing the frequency and/or intensity of contractions. "I began Pitocin this morning to speed things along, and now we're just waiting for the baby to arrive," she added.

Her contractions became stronger over the following three hours, but she didn't completely dilate. Jinger was completely dilated and pushing after 18 hours of labor. In spite of her efforts, she made almost little progress throughout labor. She pushed for 30 minutes, and out came the gorgeous baby, Felicity.

As Jinger put it, "So I had an epidural, and I was sleeping fairly comfortably as the anesthetic was being delivered during labor." I experienced pressure and pains and whatnot and wasn't sure what was going on, but I felt quite okay given that I'd already been in labor for 12 hours without that. After I regained consciousness, the nurse examined me and said, "Wow, you're dilated to 10!" And I was astonished because I was like, "How could this happen?" How did this happen? Excuse me, I was just napping! "They made me switch positions every 30 minutes, and I believe it was the key to my success."

"When it came time to push, everything seemed to just go so quickly," she added. To use a cliche, she found it "extremely fulfilling." It wasn't what she imagined it to be, of course, since she got an epidural. She thought it would be much more challenging, so she was pleasantly surprised when it all went well.

Jinger and Jeremy's daughter, Felicity, was born at 4:37 a.m. on July 19, 2018. She measured 19.5 inches in length and weighed 8 pounds, 3 ounces. Jeremy's parents, Michelle and Jana Duggar, were there, as were Jessa (Duggar) Seewald, her husband Ben, and their two boys, Spurgeon and Henry, who unexpectedly came from Texas.

After the delivery, Jeremy released a statement in which he thanked God for his kindness. Baby and mom are doing fine and getting plenty of rest. He was extremely glad for her safe birth and looked forward to life as parents!

Josh's Guilty Plea in The Child Porn Case as A "Dishonor"

Josh Duggar's family and friends still can't believe that he was found guilty of receiving and having evidence of child sexual abuse. Jinger (Duggar) Vuolo, Josh's younger sister, gave a long speech in which she criticized her brother's actions and called them "horrific and wicked."

The victims of this awful child abuse have our deepest sympathy. She said, "Our hearts go out to Josh's wife and their two beautiful children." We mourn the damage done to Christ's reputation as a result of this. Josh says he's a Christian.

She begged her fans to feel terrible for the victims and not blame the Christian religion for Josh's conduct, and the jury agreed with her; thus, Jinger commended the jury for condemning her brother. Still, in spite of the grief, they were thankful. In her words, "We praise God for being a righteous God who looks out for the weak and defenseless."

She went on to say that she likes children, particularly since they are some of the most defenseless people in the world. Because of this, sex trafficking and child abuse are among the worst atrocities in the world. God hates it because it's wicked.

Some people's reaction to finding out about a hypocritical Christian is to cast doubt on Jesus's own character. To them, a Messiah whose supposed disciples take secret pleasure in the same crimes they preach against raises serious doubts about the veracity of the claims made about him.

In light of this, the Apostle Paul rebuked religious hypocrites by saying, "The name of God is blasphemed among the Gentiles because of you" (Romans 2:24). Thus, the entire family was worried about Josh's eternal fate.

Jesus loves and cherishes children, seeing their vulnerability as a chance to protect rather than exploit (Matthew 19:14). According to Jinger, the people who had brought them down were the target of his sharpest condemnation: "It would be better for him to have a large millstone attached around his neck and to be drowned in the depths of the sea" (Matthew 18:6).

Jinger was very thankful to God for revealing Josh's sinful behavior, as well as to the justice system for its dedication to safeguarding the defenseless and punishing the wicked. They were glad for justice. For the sake of those who have been harmed, she prays for more justice, vindication, protection, and healing.

After his April 2021 arrest, 34-year-old Josh entered a not guilty plea to counts of receiving and having material for child sexual abuse. In the end, the jury found him guilty on both charges after an eight-day trial. The ex-reality star, who was accused of child abuse for his actions while he was a teenager, faces up to twenty years in jail and a $250,000 fine.

During Josh's seven-day trial, his wife Anna and his siblings Jill, Justin, Jessa, and Joy-Anna all made appearances at different times, although Jinger was noticeably absent. The husbands of both Joy-Anna and Jill were there: Austin Forsyth and Derick Dillard. Both Jill and Jessa issued comments after the judgment was announced in which they expressed their approval of the conviction.

Jim Bob, 57, and his wife Michelle spoke out following their son Josh's conviction. They vowed to do everything they could in the coming days to love and support their daughter-in-law, Anna, and their children. They love and pray for Joshua as much as they love their other children, and that will never change.

According to Jim Bob, no matter what this life throws at them as parents, they will always put their faith in God. He is both their fortification and their source of strength. Thus, they expressed appreciation to everyone for their fervent prayers.

If Josh is found guilty on both charges, he could spend up to twenty years in jail and pay up to two hundred and fifty thousand dollars in penalties. His sentence was set to start in 2022, but the exact date had not yet been decided.

Jinger Duggar Discusses Her Trouser Decision

Jinger (Duggar) Vuolo talks about how she decided to add trousers to her wardrobe after not having done so for more than twenty years. As people who watched the popular TLC show 19 Kids and Counting could see, Jinger Duggar, one of Jim Bob and Michelle Duggar's 19 daughters, wore only skirts and dresses when she was young.

Jinger Vuolo, 29, writes in her and husband Jeremy's new book, The Hope We Hold: Finding Peace in the Promises of God, that she and her sisters were raised wearing skirts and dresses since it was the norm based on Deuteronomy 22:5, which stipulates, "A woman should not wear a man's clothing." (ESV).

Wearing skirts rather than trousers was seen as fundamental to the concept of modesty in Jinger's household. But she wanted to find out for herself what the Bible had to say. Jinger relates in the book how, after her marriage to Jeremy and their subsequent move to Laredo, Texas, where he worked in ministry, she found herself with a lot of time on her hands and started digging into the Bible during her alone moments at home.

The Counting On star says, "Since Jeremy and I had begun studying Scripture together, I had become more conscious of the diverse ideas and teachings Christians held." It dawned on me that not everyone read the Bible the way I had always read it, and I was curious as to why that was. She kept studying the Bible by going to church, reading commentaries, and talking with Jeremy about what she was learning.

In the book, she writes, "Growing up, I had a set of norms that I regarded as givens." In contrast, her beliefs were shifting as she "reexamined and compared them to Scripture." Her studies led her to the conclusion that "biblical modesty is deeper and more fundamental than wearing skirts instead of trousers," as she explains in The Hope We Hold. You can be modest regardless of what you wear. The key is where your heart is.

Jinger, who sought solutions by reading the Bible because she wanted to follow what the Bible stated, says she never discovered a scripture clearly barring women from wearing trousers. Jeremy was taken off guard when Jinger asked him whether she should remain wearing just skirts and dresses.

According to him, the objective wasn't to tell her what to do or make the choice for her, but just to lead her back to Scripture. Since the first day they met, he has known that she, like himself, is eager to learn the Bible's teachings and apply them in her life. Jinger states in her book that she had no inner turmoil when she began wearing trousers for the first time since she had found assurance from the Bible and that her heart was free.

But the transition was far from simple. Jinger struggled with her belief since it was at odds with her conservative family's viewpoint. She said, "I felt upset as I feared that my parents would think I didn't respect how I was raised since I knew they genuinely cared about their views, and I didn't want to harm them now that I didn't share those convictions." Thus, she had to live in truth and follow what I thought the Bible stated.

The pair now resides in Los Angeles, where Jeremy is pursuing a Master of Divinity degree at the Master's Seminary. In March 2019, they told people about their move to Los Angeles to attend Grace Community Church and Jeremy's graduate studies at The Master's Seminary. "Through much prayer and advice, the next step for their family is to migrate to Los Angeles," according to them.

Chapter 9

THE RELEASE OF HER EXPLOSIVE NEW BOOK

Jinger Duggar Vuolo has always been the family outcast, yet she's never been mistaken for a typical James Dean type. Her upbringing was documented on the reality show "19 Kids & Counting," which chronicled the religiously devout and socially conservative Duggar family. Jinger appeared to stand out even among her 18 siblings; in one episode, she expressed a desire to leave their little rural Arkansas community and go to the big city.

Jinger followed in her family's footsteps by getting married and having kids quickly. She married Jeremy Vuolo, a former

127

professional soccer player. Jinger, however, quickly demonstrated to supporters that she was prepared to go her own way and not conform to the Duggar norm.

Jinger and her husband Jeremy are living out Jinger's ambition of an adventurous metropolitan lifestyle by relocating to Los Angeles, while the rest of her siblings have remained closer to home. She also broke the Duggar dress code, which requires women to always wear long skirts and cover their arms and upper chests, earlier than any of her sisters.

After that, Jinger moved farther and farther away from her parents. She went to a Michael Bublé concert, began collecting designer shoes, and—most surprising of all—left her childhood church to join Jeremy's. However, Jinger has yet to do her greatest act of defiance.

She is publishing a book about leaving the controversial religion of her parents, which is sure to shock the rest of the Duggar family.

An Excerpt from The Book Will Be Made Available for Free.

Becoming Free, Jinger Duggar's planned tell-all, will soon be available in its entirety. A few weeks from now isn't a long time to wait, and she's already giving us a sneak peek. Jinger has released the first chapter of her book to those who have preordered it, and even these opening pages tell a great deal about her true feelings about the way the world views her.

A Metaphor's Experience of an Existence Before One's Own Eyes.

Fans are already discussing the chapter's contents on Reddit, and it seems like Jinger dives right in, talking about how she feels like growing up on reality TV is like living in The Truman Show and how difficult it is for her to deal with so many strangers having opinions on what she should do with her life.

Her Thoughts On Freedom Not Being the Ticket to Happiness

She appreciated that others cared about her happiness, but they were wrong about what she needed to hear. In fact, Jinger made it clear in the excerpts that she does not think freedom is the way to happiness at all. One comment in particular caught the attention of fans, like Katie Joy of Without a Crystal Ball, who posted it on Instagram.

"I've realized that limitless freedom does not give birth to a happy existence." More bonding occurs as a result. Why? Since "it puts me in command of my life" and "I am not the greatest judge of what is best for me," she explained why she didn't want that.

It's hard for Jinger to settle on anything if she has an infinite number of choices and the burden of finding out what would make her genuinely happy.

Fans Are a Bit Sad for Jinger After Reading the First Chapter.

Some of Jinger's admirers who commented on Katie Joy's article were disappointed to see that, despite her efforts to distance herself from the IBLP's views, she still believes she doesn't know what's best for herself. Someone said, "She is not the greatest judge of what is best for her life." Ouch, that phrase really stings. She has not evolved beyond her misogynistic beliefs and behaviors toward women.

Someone else chimed in, "It seems like she does not have self-confidence or the courage to do the hard work and become her own person to make her own life choices."

How Much Has Jinger Progressed Since Her Childhood?

While it's difficult to get an opinion on the book based on the introduction alone, it looks like she has piqued readers' interest enough to make them want to continue reading.

Jinger has matured much since she abandoned Michelle's and Jim Bob's repressive ideas, but it seems that she still has more maturing to do. She has already accomplished a great deal, and the release of this book marks a significant milestone on her way to more success.

Jinger Duggar Vuolo Claims Her Childhood Church Was Toxic.

The religious beliefs of the Duggars have long been controversial. The Institute in Basic Life Principles (IBLP), a fundamentalist Baptist sect founded by Bill Gothard, is where the Duggars' parents, Jim Bob and Michelle, belong.

According to NBC News, Gothard pushed spouses to produce as many children as God would allow while discouraging them from participating in public schooling, dating, or even pop culture. Jinger Duggar Vuolo has written her most honest book yet, in which she says she is leaving the strict religious beliefs of her family, the Duggars.

Thomas Nelson, the Christian division of HarperCollins Publishers, releases "Becoming Free Indeed: My Story of Disentangling Faith from Fear" in January 2023. The advertising material guarantees an eye-opening analysis of the IBLP's "destructive ideology."

Even though Jinger felt that she could never live up to the church's goals, she was sure that keeping the rules was the path to success and God's favor. Ultimately,

Jinger's husband Jeremy and brother-in-law Ben Seewald encouraged her to sever relations with them permanently. Fans are curious about Jinger's connection with Michelle and Jim Bob, as well as what kind of dirt she will drop in her book.

Meanwhile, Gothard resigned from his own church in 2014 following allegations of sexual harassment within the ministry. She risks having her family permanently disown her for speaking out against their authoritarian father, just like her sister Jill Duggar Dillard did before her.

Chapter 10

FAMILY SQUABBLES AND CRITICISM

Office Offense

The viewers were shocked when Jinger showed them her chaotic workplace. The reality star shot their segment from an unidentified office space inside the larger establishment. At the start, she filmed a half-empty bookshelf with a "Master the Mess" sticker superimposed on it.

Jinger turned the camera to see a huge pile of books lying on the ground off to one side. The books looked like they had been dumped in front of a little sofa and were just waiting to be added to the empty bookcases.

Jinger gave no background information about her actions or motivations. She also remained evasive about whether she was working from home or a traditional workplace. She isn't the first Duggar family member to get into a "mess" and draw criticism.

Several of her siblings have been called out for similar transgressions.

Family Problem

Jessa Duggar, who is 30 years old, got some negative feedback after she posted a picture of her son Spurgeon doing his schoolwork in the middle of a sea of Legos. a potted plant that was hiding the infant from view while he was sitting at a desk.

Jessa said in the caption on her photo, "Too hip for school." Despite the chaos, fans were still posting photos and comments about it on Reddit. Someone's caustic comment, "That room is a disaster," stands out. To which a third party said, "It's common knowledge that children are untidy."

When asked about it, one user said, "I will never understand why she doesn't toss all that rubbish and filth into a blasted shopping bag and move it out of the image before broadcasting it to hundreds of thousands of followers."

The Duggar family as a whole, including Jill Duggar, has been under fire from the public. She told her audience she had trouble keeping up with the washing. She posted a picture of her overflowing laundry basket with the message, "Living out of here."

Is Jinger Duggar Vuolo's New Book a Dig at 19 Kids and Counting Critics?

What people said about 19 Kids and Counting may have influenced Jinger Duggar Vuolo's next book. From the time they first debuted on TLC, viewers were captivated by the larger-than-life Duggar family. But things really heated up as the Duggar children matured, got married, and left the family complex that Jim Bob and Michelle had established.

Several of the Duggar children, for example, did not adhere to their parents' conservative values. Fans speculated that Jim Bob and Michelle's influence over their older children had waned when they heard that Jinger had cut her hair short and that Anna, the Duggars' wife, wore jeans.

Jinger Duggar Vuolo's followers already have a lot of questions about her, and now she's publishing a book that may not answer any of them.

Does Jinger Duggar Vuolo Knows About Fans' Opinions?

Fans of the Duggars who began watching on TLC while Jinger was still a young adolescent will remember the "free Jinger" campaign. Early on, some viewers thought that Jinger would end up leaving the traditional Duggar family. Many of Jinger's followers held their breath when she started dating Jeremy Vuolo, a former soccer player turned preacher, in the hopes that she would finally be able to escape her parents and the burden of caring for so many younger siblings.

Jinger has made some public decisions that aren't very Duggar-like, and she's spoken out about them, but she's also made it clear that she's aware of the rumors that circulate about her. Jinger's sisters had already confirmed that they knew about the "free Jinger" campaign, which made her fans on Reddit talk about it.

As a result, some people think that Jinger's new tell-all book is both a reaction to and a result of the bad reviews.

Is Jinger's New Book's Title a Response to Duggar Family Criticism?

A "s*** post" with "top notch snarking nicely done" was reportedly the most popular remark on a Reddit thread where Duggar followers (maybe not fans) critiqued Jinger's book. This would be clear from Jinger

143

Vuolo's book, which is said to be called "Becoming Free Indeed: My Story of Untangling Faith from Fear."

Because of the "Free Jinger" campaign, many people immediately assumed that the title of Jinger's book was "Free Jinger." Jinger flipped the script on her detractors in order to give her story a more credible context. However, not everyone bought into the trolling explanation. Considering Jinger's upbringing and history as well as her husband's profession as a pastor, the theological overtones of the phrase "free indeed" were brought out in the comments.

A few commentators have suggested that it could be both. Whatever the case may be, the book has already generated considerable buzz. Most commenters on Reddit, though, agreed that the book probably won't be the juicy tell-all they're expecting.

What Is Jinger Vuolo's New Book About?

Jinger's latest book has a title that seems to say it all, but potential buyers are still unsure what it means. It is generally agreed that when Jinger discusses her religion, she will do so in the context of the ways in which her views have evolved since she was a teenager. A few users, though, are skeptical that she would really state that her parents taught her to mistrust religion.

145

At worst, it'll be a small quarrel, as one reader put it, suggesting that Jinger won't throw her parents under the bus in order to profit from the situation. However, the synopsis does provide a little more information, saying, in part, that "Jinger, together with three of her sisters, published a New York Times bestseller on their religious views."

Despite her constant anxiety that she wasn't measuring up to the lofty standards set for her, she believed that this degree of devotion would earn God's approval. At the conclusion of the synopsis, it is said, "Now with a newfound faith and personal conviction, Becoming Free Indeed describes what it was like to live under Bill Gothard's teachings, how the Bible's truth changed her mind, and how she untangled her faith while still believing in Jesus."

It's up in the air what, if anything, the book's last pages will show fans and reviewers. Jinger's book, "Becoming Free Indeed: My Story of Disentangling Faith from Fear," will be released in January 2023.

Chapter 11

JINGER BEING IGNORED BY HER FAMILY BEFORE HER BOOK RELEASE

On her 29th birthday, about a month before her new book, Becoming Free Indeed: My Story of Untangling Faith from Fear, came out, Jinger Vuolo (formerly Jinger Duggar) received no attention from her family.

On her 29th birthday, Jinger did not get any public birthday greetings from the Duggar family. Jim Bob and Michelle Duggar have a shared Instagram account where they periodically write about major milestones; however, they neglected to mention Jinger's birthday. None of her sibling group of 18 shared news of the celebration online.

Jinger's husband, Jeremy Vuolo, however, took the time to make his wife feel special by publishing a touching tribute to her on Instagram. He posted a picture of the Counting On alumna laughing, writing, "Happy birthday to this gorgeous lady." "Aw, @jingervuolo, you know I feel the same way about you." Jinger, who is 29 and has two kids with her husband Jeremy, said, "Aww, thank you, baby!"

She also used Instagram Stories to show off birthday wishes from friends and fans, although no one from her immediate family was included.

Jinger turned 29 on December 21, 2022, and she is now promoting her new book,

Becoming Free Indeed, which is scheduled for publication on January 31, 2023. The book's summary says that the author talks about how she started to question the harmful ideas she was taught as a child and how she found true freedom in Christ.

In a November 2022 YouTube video titled "The Hardest Thing I've Ever Done," she discusses the book and explains that it is not a "tell-all about her family" but rather an exploration into her spiritual journey. Jinger will talk about why she didn't agree with Bill Gothard, the pastor at the Institute in Basic Life Principles (IBLP), and his "wrong" teachings.

An anonymous source told Touch that Jinger's parents are getting ready for the book's release after Jinger said she was writing one. "Jim Bob and Michelle aren't very excited about Jinger's book being published, but they are keeping their fingers crossed," the insider said. They have prayed about it and hope that it is honest, polite, and doesn't dig up too much of their family difficulties, but they don't know what themes she'll touch.

According to the source, Jim Bob, 57, and Michelle, 56, "fear the worst" about what Jinger would disclose in the book, particularly the "dark Josh episode" and anecdotes about their religion and raising their huge family. This is the last thing they want, the insider said: "more negative attention and scrutiny."

Even though she says the book isn't about her or her family, the star of 19 Kids and Counting is sure to talk about the Duggars' recent scandals, such as Josh Duggar's conviction for child molestation and subsequent jail time for child pornography, which all happened in 2015.

Is Her Book, "Not A Tell-All," About Her Famous Family?

Instead, the reality star's spiritual journey, or, as she puts it, her "separation of faith from fear," will be chronicled in Becoming Free Indeed. The very mention of the term "duggar" is enough to spark debate. Jim-Bob and Michelle Duggar have been the focus of interest, amazement, scrutiny, worry, and, at times, disdain since becoming public celebrities recognized for their massive offspring with a series of TLC TV specials.

This book, Vuolo says in a video she and her husband Jeremy released on YouTube, is the toughest thing she has ever had to accomplish, but it is the most necessary. She admits that, although nobody saw when the TV cameras were rolling in regards to her family, her book is more about her spiritual journey and disentangling faith from fear than a tell-all.

She said the inspiration struck in 2017 when she saw several of her friends, who were reared with the same or similar very orthodox Christian ideas, abandon not just their upbringing but Christianity altogether. They had rejected everything they had been taught about God, the Bible, and the Christian religion, she said.

According to Jinger, that's not her tale, but like those pals, she rejected a lot of the lessons she was given throughout the course of her life. She believes the same things, but she believes them differently.

The intended audience for Vuolo's book is those who have suffered harm at the hands of any religious leader who claimed to speak for God but didn't and who want to reexamine their religion without giving it up.

The controversial clergyman and founder of the Institute in Basic Life Principles (IBLP) is the subject of Vuolo's discussion. The Duggars' values and beliefs were profoundly influenced by Gothard's strict hierarchy that places men above women and other ultra-conservative teachings. In the past few years, Gothard's reputation has taken a hit because a number of women have accused him of sexual misconduct.

After years of promoting IBLP events, the Duggar family has lately tried to distance themselves from both Gothard and the institute, which has been labeled by many as a cult. Fans of the Duggar family news page "Pickles4Truth" on Facebook suspect that the timing of the memoir is not coincidental. The Duggar family will play a major role in a new Amazon documentary series.

According to administrator Diane Nevins, "I smell damage control from the Vuolos" in the autobiography. They had no choice but to flee from all of that mayhem. Vuolo's religious differences with her parents and several of her siblings have grown more obvious in recent years.

She now dresses more provocatively than she did as a youngster by wearing slacks, for instance, and she often participates in holiday traditions with her daughters, Felicity and Evangeline. As for how she gets along with her relatives at the moment, she hasn't said anything.

When her brother Josh Duggar was found guilty of child pornography in 2021, she spoke out against him. She blasted his actions as "horrific wickedness" and branded him a hypocrite. According to the book's Amazon page, her brother-in-law, who did not grow up in the Gothard and IBLP spheres, was another factor that made her question her previous convictions.

Her brother claimed to be dedicated to the Bible but disagreed with many of the teachings that Vuolo had previously accepted blindly. "It's difficult to even entertain the idea that what you were taught may have been incorrect when you grow up in a close-knit society where everyone thinks the same things about everything," she said in her video.

But is it necessary for everyone to do it nonetheless?

Her Dark Times Experience in The News

Jinger Vuolo, previously Duggar, grew up in the public eye, courtesy of reality TV series like "19 Kids and Counting" and "Counting On." Despite the fact that both of her reality shows on TLC have since been canceled, the 29-year-old mother of two recalls what it was like to have her personal life thrust into the spotlight.

According to Jinger, there are many advantages to being a celebrity. She believes a lot of people do look at fame, and they think it's all lovely and fantastic. Jinger stated on the Dinner Party podcast with Jeremy Fall, "But you also have to cope with a lot." They can assume, "Oh, you don't battle with anything; you don't battle with being melancholy one day."

In her own words, "I believe it's been more tough for me personally to find out how to go beyond that and how to actually open up to others." She elaborated, saying, "We do all experience these emotions; we have periods when we are traveling through extremely tough, deep, dark times, and other people may not know about it or they may not realize that it is something that is universal to all of us humans."

Jinger claims that her religious beliefs have helped her tremendously, both on and off camera. "We all face adversity and hardship in our lives, and it is something I think about for us," she said in the podcast episode released on July 1, 2022. "I guess for me, at those moments when I struggle the most, I simply rush to God," said a member of the religious group.

Jinger's family started shooting a documentary for the Discovery Health

Channel when she was only 10 years old, giving her a taste of reality television for the first time. A revised version, titled "19 Kids and Counting," ran on ABC from 2008 through 2015. Jinger claims that she and her family were completely taken aback by the success of their television adaptation.

They had no idea how long it would go on, according to her. Jinger anticipated it would last a year at most and produce just one documentary, but it has continued on indefinitely. And the family rapidly learned that it was difficult to trust individuals because of the influx of unpleasant comments and misleading headlines.

"I don't believe even my parents understood at first," Jinger said. People's ability to express themselves at a high level was lost on them. It was difficult to embrace the possibility that "some individuals out there are not aiming for your better benefit," she concluded.

Printed in Great Britain
by Amazon

21592838R00095